TURQUOISE MOSAICS FROM MEXICO

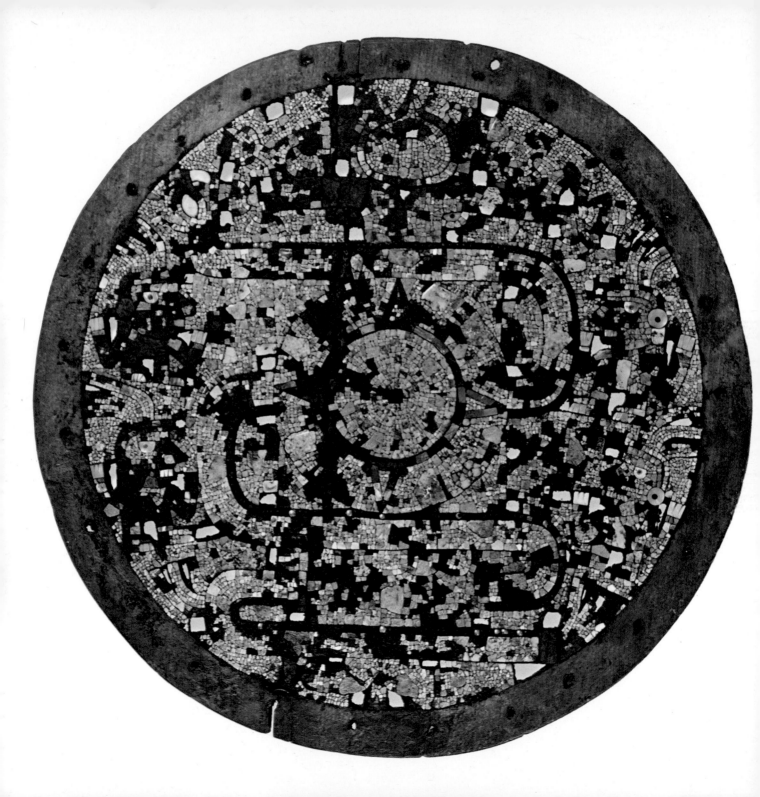

Elizabeth Carmichael

TURQUOISE MOSAICS FROM MEXICO

Published by the Trustees of the British Museum London 1970

Illustration on half title

A lapidary instructs his son. The Aztecs attributed the origin of such skilled crafts to the ancient Toltecs who had lived long before them in the Valley of Mexico, and particularly to the god-king of the Toltecs, Quetzalcoatl Ce Acatl. Much of the fine goldsmith and lapidary work was in fact probably that of Mixtec craftsmen, and either acquired by the Aztecs as tribute exacted from towns within the empire, by trade, or from Mixtec craftsmen living within Tenochtitlan or neighbouring Valley towns. Bernal Díaz describes the lapidaries in the town of Azcapotzalco, close to Tenochtitlan: 'Moctezuma employed skilled workmen in every craft that was practised among them. We will begin with the lapidaries and workers in gold and silver and all the hollow work, which even the great goldsmiths in Spain were forced to admire, and of these there were a great number in a town named Azcapotzalco, a league from Mexico. Then for working precious stones and chalchihuites (jades), which are like emeralds, there were other great artists.' There are lengthy descriptions in the *History of the Things of New Spain* of Fray Bernardino de Sahagun, of lapidary work, the gods of the lapidaries and their special festivals.
Codex Mendoza.

Frontispiece

Shields of turquoise mosaic work are very frequently listed in the inventories of booty sent to Europe at the time of the Conquest. This wooden plaque with its elaborate scene in mosaic work was probably the centre of such a shield. The holes around the edge would have served to hold in place an edging of feather work and possibly gold ornament.

The design represents a tree, with a calendar disc set at its centre; a serpent is twined about the tree. Four warriors are ranged – two on either side of the tree. A fifth figure is contained within the lozenge shape held by the branches of the tree where they bifurcate at the top of the panel. The body of the serpent was originally picked out with an edging of simulated gold beads modelled in the resinous gum used to hold the mosaic in position, and then gilded. A little of this original gilding can still be seen.

Moreover: sixteen shields of stone mosaic work, with their coloured featherwork hanging from the edge of them . . .
Report of the Jewels, Shields, and Clothing sent to the Emperor Charles V from Don Fernando Cortés and the Town Council of Vera Cruz

Contents and illustrations

I also saw the things that were brought to the King from the new land of gold: a sun entirely of gold, a whole fathom wide, and a moon entirely of silver, of equal size, likewise two rooms of rare accoutrements, of all manner of their weapons, armour, bows and arrows, wonderful arms, strange garments, bed hangings and all manner of wonderful things for many uses, all much fairer to behold than any marvel. These things are all so precious that they are valued at one hundred thousand guilders. And in all the days of my life I have seen nothing that has so rejoiced my heart as these things. For I saw among them strange and exquisitely worked objects and marvelled at the subtle genius of the men in distant lands. The things I saw there I have no words to express.

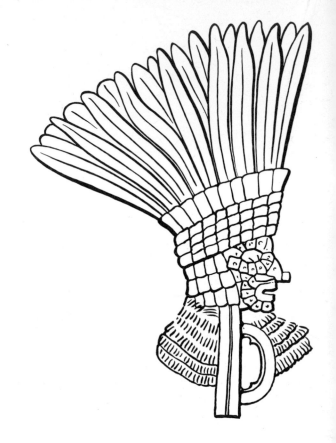

Albrecht Dürer
Brussels 1521. Extract from a diary kept during a journey in the Low Countries. July 1520 – July 1521.

Warrior wearing headdress and mosaic mask
From a relief sculpture from the Great Ball Court, Chichén Itzá

INTRODUCTION

The group of nine turquoise mosaics from Mexico in the collections of the British Museum are quite rightly considered one of the most important treasures of the Department of Ethnography. They are in themselves compelling enough visually to require no written encouragement to excite interest in them. Their probable history as some of the first examples of Mexican art to be seen by European eyes, is surely enough to sustain such interest if one imagines them in the context of the early sixteenth century in the Old World.

At the time of the Spanish Conquest of Mexico in 1519, Henry VIII was on the throne of England; Leonardo da Vinci died in that same year. Albrecht Dürer was visiting Brussels at the time when the first treasures sent home by Hernan Cortés to the Emperor Charles V were to be seen there. In an all too tantalizingly brief entry in his journal he expressed his astonishment at these things from the New World, and the way in which they moved him. The skull mask in the British Museum is said to have come from a Belgian collection; perhaps it was one of the pieces seen by Dürer.

Even without the feather work and gold ornaments which belonged with them, the masks in the collection, particularly, retain most of the impact they were obviously intended to have. They represent gods, and the vivid colour, the startling contrast of the bared white teeth against the blue of the turquoise, the sheen, and in moving light, even the glitter, of the stones all combine to convince one that, placed over the faces of human beings dressed in all the rich garments and regalia and with the tall, elaborate feather headdresses of Aztec priests, the effect must have been magnificent and somewhat terrifying.

The complexity of Mexican civilization in the Aztec period, and the vast literature on most aspects of it, make it impossible to describe adequately here. The lengthy history of the building of the Aztec empire, the highly complex religions of the Valley of Mexico at that time and the events of the Spanish Conquest have all filled many books. A short bibliography at the end of this text suggests a few general works to provide a background as well as listing books of special interest in connection with the turquoise mosaics.

It is hoped that as a result of work currently in progress at the British Museum it will be possible to devote a subsequent publication to the materials and technology of the turquoise mosaics in the collections. A good deal is known of lapidary work in the Aztec period from post-Conquest accounts, and this may best be treated at that time. By far the greatest number of turquoise mosaic decorated items found in Mexico (predominantly masks and shields), have come from Oaxaca. However, fine examples of mosaic work have also been found at the post-Classic Maya site of Chichén Itzá in northern Yucatán. Warriors wearing mosaic masks are depicted on relief carvings at that site, and although the masks they wear may not be made of turquoise, they do illustrate well how the combined mask and headdress looked when worn.

THE CONQUEST OF MEXICO

How the turquoise mosaics and other Aztec treasures came to Europe

In the museums of Europe exist a few treasured objects which form a tiny remnant of the rich bounty brought across the Atlantic at the time of the Spanish Conquest of Mexico. Some were sent back as part of the tribute due to the Emperor Charles V, and some came with the personal booty of the *conquistadores*. It is a matter for lament that more of the precious objects described in the inventories of the period have not survived: the exquisite textiles, intricate gold work, elaborate feather mosaics, the many jewels and ornaments, plumed head-dresses, etc., have nearly all disappeared.[1] It seems likely that in many instances the intrinsic value to Europeans of the materials employed in their manufacture must have overridden any appreciation of the craftsmanship and style of the objects. Not everyone was as excited by the workmanship of the unknown artists from the New World as were the German painter Albrecht Dürer and, reputedly, the Italian goldsmith, Benvenuto Cellini.[2] Thus many irreplaceable examples of Mexican art were melted down, or re-worked and the precious stones which had ornamented them placed in new settings.[3]

Other items, like the textiles and feather mosaic work, had no better chance of survival in the European treasure houses than they would have had in their native land. Feather mosaic work was one of the most highly developed skills of the Mexican craftsmen. Detailed descriptions and fascinating illustrations of the production of shields, hangings and other items ornamented with feather mosaic are given in post-Conquest accounts.[4] Sadly, of the many examples brought to Europe, only a handful have resisted destruction by insects and natural decay. The most famous examples are the splendid quetzal feather headdress, the standard and the shield preserved in the Museum für Völkerkunde in Vienna.

Among the objects considered of less intrinsic value, and which have fortunately not proved so fragile, are examples of turquoise and shell mosaic work. These excited interest on account of their exotic forms and origins as well as for the perfection with which the mosaic was executed. As Peter Martyr says,

We also admire the artistically made masks. The *superstructure* is of wood, covered over with stones, so artistically and perfectly joined together that it is impossible to detect their lines of junction with the fingernail. They seem to the naked eye to be one single stone. . . . These masks are placed upon the faces of the gods, whenever the sovereign is ill, not to be removed until he either recovers or dies.[5]

These, along with some of the painted books, carved wooden objects, jades, etc., were dispersed throughout Europe where, in private collections and cabinets of curiosities, they were, to all intents and purposes, lost. In the nineteenth century there was a revival of interest in ancient Mexico which inspired museum curators and private collectors to seek them out.

The British Museum is indebted to one such, the textile manufacturer, Henry Christy. A chance meeting

Portrait of Hernan Cortés
From an oil painting in the Hospital de
Jesus Nazareno, City of Mexico.

with the anthropologist Edward Tylor, when both were travelling in Cuba, led Christy to undertake a journey to Mexico. From that time on, inspired by what he saw, he collected antiquities from Mexico. The first turquoise mosaics acquired by the British Museum were those which Christy had purchased at the sale of the collections of a Mr Bram Hertz. The mosaics (the skull mask, the mask thought to represent Quetzalcoatl or Tonatiuh and the sacrificial knife) came to the Museum with the rest of his collection of ethnography and antiquities after his death in 1865. (See Appendix A.) Six other turquoise mosaic decorated items were added to the British Museum's collections between 1865 and 1894. The total collection of nine items is the largest in Europe and accounts for approximately one-third of the mosaics so far discovered which are thought to have come to Europe shortly after the Conquest.

The story of the Conquest of Mexico is well documented and many excellent accounts are readily available. Probably the best of these are the letters sent to Charles V by the *conquistador* Hernan Cortés between 1519 and 1526 and the work of his follower, Bernal Díaz del Castillo.[6] Bernal Díaz had also taken part in the earlier voyage of discovery which set out from Cuba under the leadership of Juan de Grijalva in 1518. In the same year his ships had landed on the Mexican coast and it was from this expedition that the first examples of mosaic work are recorded. From the Indians of Potonchan, Tabasco, San Juan de Ulúa and 'other places along the coast' Grijalva obtained by trade quite a large collection of objects in gold including: 'small hollow idols',

Figure wearing a skull as part of his costume
Codex Zouche Nuttall

This mask, based upon a human skull, is thought to represent the god Tezcatlipoca, one of the most important Aztec gods, with a long history in the Valley of Mexico. His name which means 'Smoking Mirror', is derived from the Nahuatl word *tezcapoctli*, 'shining smoke', the soot with metallic flecks used to paint the face of images of the god. Along with Quetzalcoatl, Tezcatlipoca was considered one of the creator gods to whom the supreme being, *nelli teotl*, 'the true god', considered to be a dual male-female principle, Ometecuhtli and Omecíhuatl, 'Lord and Lady of Duality', had entrusted the creation of the lesser gods, the world and men. However Quetzalcoatl and Tezcatlipoca often appear as adversaries, opposed forces of light and darkness, good and evil. As Lord of the night sky and the Great Bear, Tezcatlipoca is the patron of highwaymen and sorcerers, also of warriors and the young men who were trained in the *Telpochcalli,* the school of war for those who were not of noble birth. In the codices he can be identified by the obsidian mirrors, one at the temple and one in place of a foot torn off by the earth monster; also by the black bands at forehead, nose and chin. In the obsidian mirror he can see all things; he is omnipotent, omnipresent, 'like the darkness, like the mind'.

Writing of this mask in his book *Anahuac*, Edward Tylor says: 'The mixture of art, civilization, and barbarism which the hideous aspect of this green and black skull-mask presents accords with the condition of Mexico at the time of the Conquest, under which human sacrifices on a gigantic scale were coincident with much refinement in arts and manners.' This, written in 1861, when the ancient civilizations of Mexico were not well understood, and Mexican art appreciated rather for its exoticism than for any of its truer merits, nonetheless touches upon a conflict in Aztec civilization which more recent scholars have been concerned to express: 'Aztec religion, on the mystico-militaristic level, sought to preserve the life of the Sun . . . through ceremonial warfare and human sacrifice. The supreme ideal of the Aztec warriors was to fulfil their mission as the chosen people of Tonatiuh, the Sun, who needed the precious liquid if he were to continue to shine over *Cemanáhuac*, the world. At the same time, however, many of the wise men, living in the shadow of the great symbol of Nahuatl wisdom, Quetzalcoatl, attempted to discover the meaning of life on an intellectual plane. These almost diametrically opposed attitudes toward life and the universe existed side by side – a situation similar to that of Nazi Germany in our time, where a mystico-militaristic world view and a genuinely humanistic philosophy and literature coexisted. Indeed, such a mixture of humanism and barbarism seems to be an inherent quality of the so-called rational animal' (León-Portilla).

Skulls of sacrificial victims were placed on the *tzompantli* or 'skull rack', which in Tenochtitlan was located in the precinct of the Great Temple. Sometimes the skulls were included in offerings, with, as is often seen in the codices, stone blades projecting from the nasal cavity and from the mouth. Also in the codices people are seen wearing skull ornaments as part of their costume. The extremely long leather straps on the skull mask in the British Museum collection would certainly make it possible to wear it in this way.

The God Tezcatlipoca, he was considered a true god, invisible, able to enter everywhere, in the heavens, on earth and into the place of the dead. It was said that when he was upon earth he incited people to war, created enmity and discord and caused much anguish and disquiet. He set people against one another so that they made wars, and for this reason he was called 'the enemy on both sides'.

He alone understood how the world was governed, and alone gave prosperity and riches, and took them away at will; he gave riches, prosperity and fame, courage and command, dignities and honour, and took them away again as he willed. For this he was feared and reverenced, for it was within his power to raise up or to cast down. . . .

Sahagun, *History of the Things of New Spain*, Bk 1.

a 'gold helmet with two horns and black hair', several mirrors, shields and many other things. Listed in an inventory of the items are the following:

four gilded wooden masks, one inlaid with two straight bands of turquoise;
another with ears of the same, although with more gold;
another inlaid in the same way from the nose up;
a fourth, from the eyes up;
one dog's head covered with little stones;
seven flint sacrificial knives.[7]

We also have a record of the things traded for this rich hoard – a rather tawdry collection of 'kerchiefs . . . coarse linen shirts . . . glass beads and medallions . . . combs and needles'.

In the following year, after Grijalva's return, Hernan Cortés set out on an expedition to these newly discovered lands 'having ten caravels, and four hundred men at arms, amongst whom were many knights and other noblemen, and sixteen horses'.[8]

The great Aztec ruler, Moctezuma, had heard of the landing of Grijalva; reports had come to him of the 'mountains that moved' on the sea, which is how his informant described the Spanish ships. And in San Juan de Ulúa, Cortés heard from Indians and in particular from the local dignitary, Teudilli, of Moctezuma, who was 'no less a king' than the Emperor Charles V whom Cortés said had sent him to their land, 'and no less good; rather it was astonishing to learn that there could be in the world such another great prince'.

Cortés was soon to find, however, that Moctezuma had enemies enough, especially among the coastal peoples of Mexico. People like the Tlaxcalans who were willing to form an alliance with the Spaniards in the hope of overthrowing the Aztec king in his great city of Tenochtitlan built upon Lake Texcoco in the Valley of Mexico. When Cortés marched inland to meet Moctezuma he had augmented his small force from among the Indian groups anxious to bring to an end the exacting demands from Tenochtitlan for tribute and for sacrificial victims.

Cortés, Díaz and others of the *conquistadores*, Andres de Tapia, Francisco de Aguilar and the so-called 'anonymous conqueror', have left vivid accounts of what they saw and encountered on that march inland and their first contacts with the great Aztec civilization. Reading them we are able to share some of their excitement and wonder, and also sometimes, their horror at what they saw. Díaz wrote of the approach towards Tenochtitlan:

We arrived at a broad causeway . . . and when we saw so many cities and villages built in the water and other great towns on dry land and that straight and level causeway going towards Mexico, we were amazed and said that it was like the enchantments they tell of in the legend of Adamis, on account of the great towers and temples and buildings rising from the water, and all built of masonry. And some of our soldiers even asked whether the things they saw were not a dream?

Cortés describes as follows the effigies of the gods to whom some of this glory was dedicated:

The figures of the idols, in which those people believe, exceed in size the body of a large man. They are made of a mass of all the seeds and vegetables which they eat, ground up and mixed with one another, and kneaded with the hearts' blood of human beings, whose breasts are opened when alive, the hearts being removed, and, with the blood which comes out, is kneaded the flour, making

The Aztecs practised several forms of human sacrifice, but the most characteristic one was the removal of the heart from a living victim. There are many scenes of such sacrifices in the codices, where the sacrificing priest is seen plunging the knife into the breast of a victim thrown onto his back across a stone and held by assisting priests. Sacrifice of this kind was thought to be a necessity if the sun was to be kept moving in its course. In the legend concerning the creation of the sun at Teotihuacan, it is said that at first the sun was still in the heavens; it would not move until all the gods who had helped in the creation had been sacrificed to provide the vital blood to set it on its way. The death of the gods had made possible the life and movement of the sun, but to maintain that life and movement, it was the duty of man to provide nourishment by continual blood sacrifice.

The handle of this knife is in the form of a crouching 'Eagle Knight', whose face is seen in the open beak of a headdress in the form of an eagle's head; the wings cloak his shoulders. He wears a nose ornament of malachite. *Quauhtli*, 'eagle', was the other name for Tonatiuh, the sun; it is appropriate therefore that the sacrificial knife should show an 'Eagle Knight' and that the offering dish in which the human hearts were placed should be called *quauhxicalli* or 'eagle vessel'. In the 'Sacred War' which was instituted to provide sacrificial victims, warriors who attained the great honour of becoming 'Eagle' or 'Jaguar' knights (the jaguar was the *alter ego* of Tezcatlipoca the god of darkness) were those most dedicated to the cause of feeding the sun

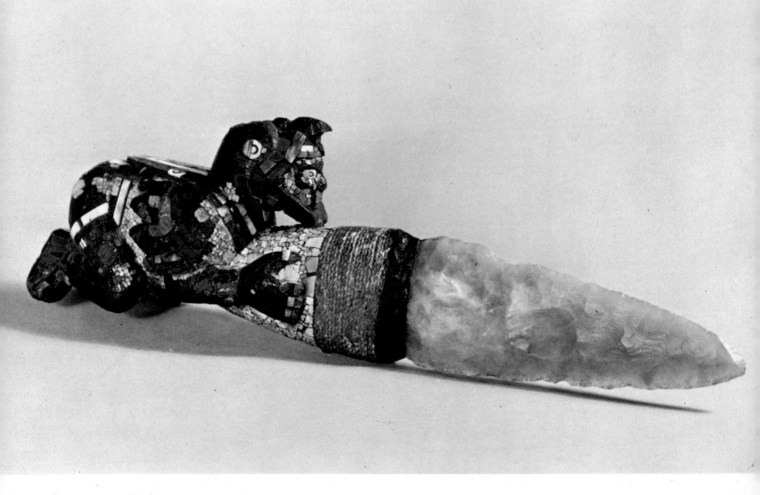

by sacrifice, symbolizing in their conflict the opposing forces of light and darkness. At the important ceremony in honour of the sun on the day '4 Motion', the day on which tradition said the present age (the fifth) of the world would end, special sacrifice was made, and dances were performed with the military orders dressed in their full regalia.

The beautiful mosaic work on this piece continues on the reverse side of the heads only, the rest of the body being set upon a hollowed-out wooden backing. The holes at the top of the inner loops of the serpent body suggest that it was worn suspended, perhaps as a pectoral ornament. The now empty eye sockets would possibly have been set with eyes of shell and polished discs of iron pyrites as in the case of the skull mask and small animal head.

the quantity necessary to construct a great statue. When these are finished the priests offer them more hearts, which have likewise been sacrificed, and besmear the faces with the blood.

The intensive work of recent years upon the surviving manuscripts in the Nahuatl language of the Aztecs, for which Spanish missionaries introduced a written form using roman characters not long after the Conquest, has given us a better understanding of the impact upon the Mexicans of their first sudden and violent contact with Europeans. The pale-skinned and bearded men dressed in strange clothes were first reported to Moctezuma as coming from 'a mountain range or small mountain floating in the midst of the water'. They sometimes mounted upon the backs of animals which seemed to the Aztecs to resemble deer:

Their deer carry them on their backs wherever they wish to go. These deer are as tall as the roof of a house. . . . As for their food, it is like human food. It is large and white, and not heavy. It is something like straw, but with the taste of a cornstalk. . . . Their dogs are enormous, with flat ears and long, dangling tongues. The colour of their eyes is a burning yellow; their eyes flash fire and shoot off sparks. Their bellies are hollow, their flanks long and narrow. They are tireless and very powerful. They bound here and there, panting, with their tongues hanging out. And they are spotted like an ocelot.

The same messengers, returning from their meeting with Cortés also told of the terrifying cannon which had caused them to faint and temporarily deafened them:

A thing like a ball of stone comes out of its entrails: it comes out shooting sparks and raining fire. . . . If the cannon is aimed against a mountain, the mountain splits and cracks open. If it is aimed against a tree, it shatters the tree into splinters. This is a most unnatural sight, as if the tree had exploded from within.

Plan of the city of Tenochtitlan attributed to Cortés, showing the Great Temple complex at the centre of the city, the town itself and some of the outlying settlements. It was originally published in Nuremburg in a Latin edition of some of the *Cartas de Relacion* – the reports sent by Cortés to the Emperor Charles V during the Conquest of Mexico.

 1 The Iztapalapan Causeway
 2 The Fort Xoloc
 3 Houses and Gardens of Moctezuma in the outskirts
 4 Plaza
 5 The New palace of Moctezuma
 6 The Palace gardens
 7 The Menagerie
 8 The Serpent Wall around the temple enclosure
 9 The Market-place at Tlatelolco
10 The Nonoalco Causeway, leading to Tacuba
11 Causeway leading to Tenayuca
12 The Tlacopan Causeway
13 Chapultepec, the Park
14 Chapultepec, the Springs
15 Quays for canoes plying across the lake towards Texcoco and eastwards
16 Dike to prevent flooding of the city
17 Canals with wooden bridges
18 Idol, decapitated and thrown down
19 Temple
20 House near which the Spaniards were ambushed

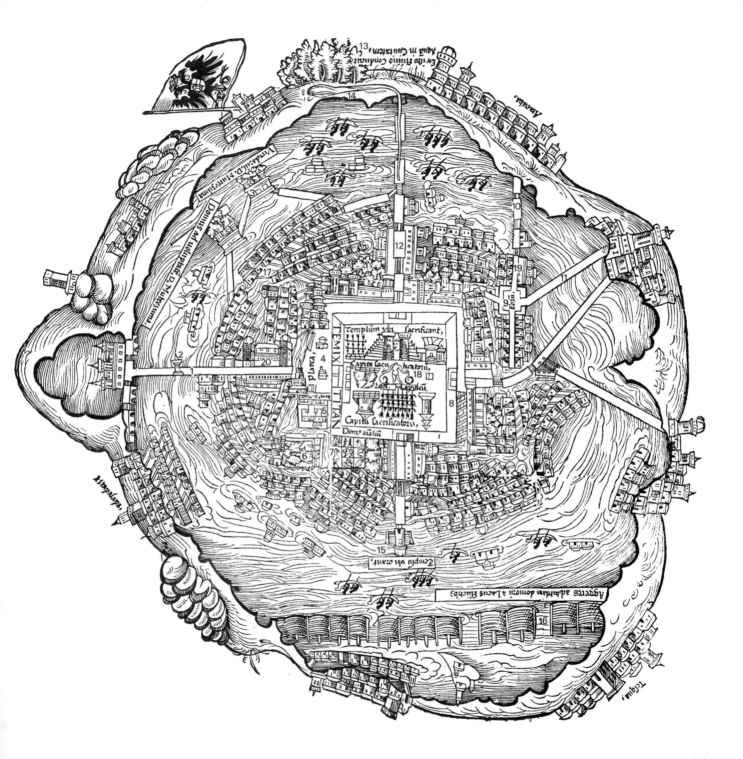

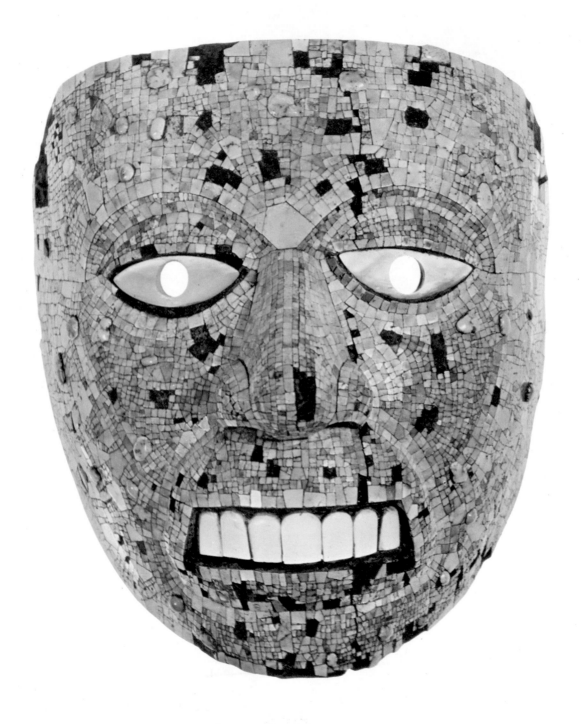

This mask, usually thought to represent the god Quetzalcoatl, is one of the best preserved examples of Mexican turquoise mosaic work. The mosaic is set with resinous gum over a wooden matrix. The eyes are of pearl shell and the teeth of white shell. We know that at certain festivals and upon the death of a king masks were placed over the faces of effigies of the gods, and that they were placed upon the dead dressed for burial. Sahagun describes the dressing of Cortés in the regalia of the god Quetzalcoatl, including the information that 'they put on him the turquoise mosaic serpent' mask. The circular holes in the inset eyes of this mask suggest that it was in fact to be worn, probably by the priests during ceremonies devoted to the god represented.

It has been suggested that this mask might represent the sun, Tonatiuh. The Aztec story of the creation of the sun tells that the gods gathered at Teotihuacan, and a small leprous god, whose face was covered with boils, threw himself into a great fire, and arose from it as the sun. Possibly the large irregularly shaped turquoises which are a feature of this mask might represent the boils on the face of Tonatiuh.

If the mask does however represent Quetzalcoatl, it is a fit tribute to the god-king of Toltec times, Quetzalcoatl Ce Acatl who during the course of his glorious reign in Tula was credited with having introduced many of the arts still practised in the Aztec period:

The Toltecs, the people of Quetzalcoatl, were very skilful.

Nothing was difficult for them to do.
They cut precious stones,
wrought gold,
and made many works of art
and marvelous ornaments of feathers.
Truly they were skilful.

All the arts of the Toltecs,
their knowledge, everything came from Quetzalcoatl.

Anales de Cuauhtitlán

It is scarcely surprising that after such a recital we should be told that

when Moctezuma heard this report, he was filled with terror. It was as if his heart had fainted, as if it had shrivelled. It was as if he were conquered by despair.

This image of Moctezuma as from the first overwhelmed by the arrival of the invaders pervades the accounts of the Conquest. It was not merely his sense that against such weapons the Aztec *maquauhuitl*, the club edged with sharp blades of obsidian, would be of little use; nor was it the obvious terrifying resolve in battle shown by the Spaniards (they had cause, since all but one of the ships which had brought them to Mexico had been destroyed, and for them there was no return, only conquest or death); it was an extraordinary accident of history. The native historians tell us that the arrival of Cortés came at the end of a ten-year period filled with strange omens and portents of evil: a comet had appeared in the sky 'shaped like a flaming ear of corn'; the temple of the Aztec tribal god Huitzilopochtli had burst into flames without any fire being set to it; the waters of the lake upon which their city was built had suddenly foamed up and flooded the buildings; a strange bird was caught with a mirror set in its head. Gazing into this mirror Moctezuma saw first the night sky although at the time it was broad daylight, and when he looked again, he saw a

distant plain. People were moving across it, spread out in ranks and coming forward in great haste. They made war upon each other and rode upon the backs of animals which resembled deer.

There is little doubt that even before the landing of Grijalva, Moctezuma had heard rumours of strange invaders in the east. This must have caused him some unease. Also, the ruler of such a large empire whose reign had constantly been troubled by wars and rebellions could never have felt truly secure. He was by nature a scholarly and reserved king, renowned for his knowledge of religions and proud of the inheritance of Toltec learning and refinement which the Aztecs prized so highly. It was this deep concern and belief in the Toltec traditions which was the most important factor in his reaction to the coming of Cortés. These traditions told that the priest-king of the Toltecs (the great people who had long ago ruled the Valley of Mexico from their city of Tula) – Quetzalcoatl Ce Acatl Topiltzin, 'Feathered Serpent, One Reed, our venerated Lord', who had over the years become identified with the great god, Quetzalcoatl, whose name he bore – would one day return to claim the throne from which he had been driven; to rule once more over his people. In Tula, Quetzalcoatl had renounced human sacrifice and set himself in opposition to the rites associated with the god Tezcatlipoca. By the sorcery of Tezcatlipoca and his followers he was driven from Tula after a twenty-year reign marked by great advances in the arts and learning: a 'golden age' which the Aztecs still looked to centuries later as the time of origin for all fine craftsmanship. Quetzalcoatl was described in the legends as pale-skinned and bearded; and, moreover, he had promised to return from his journey to the distant lands in the east in the year *ce acatl*, one reed. The year of Cortés's landing, 1519, corresponded in the Aztec calendar to the year *ce acatl*.

Although Moctezuma seems fatalistically to have accepted that Cortés must be the god Quetzalcoatl, it did not prevent him from trying to turn him and his companions away from Tenochtitlan both by persuasion and by the sorcery of his priests. However, each failure of their magic merely strengthened Moctezuma's belief in the superhuman powers of the invaders. Although he seems to have been at first almost afraid to encounter the supposed god, he was anxious to be correct in serving him, and immediately sent messengers bearing the costumes and regalia appropriate to Quetzalcoatl. The following description comes from the *General History of the Things of New Spain* of Fray Bernardino de Sahagun:

[Moctezuma] said to them: 'Come, O ye intrepid warriors; come! it is said that our Lord [Queztalcoatl] hath at last arrived. Receive him. Listen sharply; lend your ears well to what he will say. You will bring back what is well heard. Behold wherewith you will arrive before our lord.'
First was the array of Quetzalcoatl: a serpent mask made of turquoise mosaic; a quetzal feather head fan; a plaited neckband of precious green stone beads, in the midst of which lay a golden disc; and a shield with bands of gold crossing each other or with bands of gold crossing other bands of sea shells, with spread quetzal feathers about the lower edge and with a quetzal feather flag; and a mirror upon the small of the back, with quetzal feathers, and this mirror for the small of the back was like a turquoise shield, of turquoise mosaic—encrusted with turquoise, glued with turquoise; and green stone neck bands, on which were golden shells; and then the turquoise spear thrower, which had on it only turquoise with a sort of serpent's head; it had the head of a serpent, and obsidian sandals.

He also sent the masks and costumes of the gods Tezcatlipoca and Tlaloc, as well as many baskets of treasures for the gods. The Spaniards had made no

Scene of human sacrifice using a stone-
bladed knife
Codex Zouche Nuttall

secret of their desire for gold and other precious objects; no doubt Moctezuma had heeded their words. It is often supposed that some of the turquoise mosaic pieces now in the British Museum were part of that first gift of Moctezuma to Cortés, given in the mistaken belief that he was the god Quetzalcoatl. Part of the offering was certainly sent back to Charles V in Europe, for shortly after the visit of the ambassadors from Tenochtitlan, Cortés

Messengers from Moctezuma bearing gifts to Cortés
Florentine Codex

in order to conciliate his master's goodwill . . . proposed to send him such a present as should suggest lofty ideas of the importance of his own services to the crown. To effect this, the royal fifth he considered inadequate. He conferred with his officers, and persuaded them to relinquish their share of the treasure. At his instance, they made a similar application to the soldiers; representing that it was the earnest wish of the general, who set the example by resigning his own fifth, equal to the share of the crown.[9]

The masks in the British Museum collection can be considered to correspond reasonably well with those described for the gods, although the iconography is by no means always certain. Unfortunately the inventories of the treasures made in Vera Cruz and in Europe are couched in somewhat vague terms; masks might have been treated as parts of the several headdresses listed, as well as separately. There is a further description given by Sahagun's informants of how a 'quetzal feather head-fan went with the serpent mask': the messengers from Moctezuma were taken aboard the boat of Cortés;

they bore in their arms the array of the gods . . . they adorned the Captain himself; they put on him the turquoise mosaic serpent mask; with it went the quetzal feather head fan; and . . . the green stone ear plugs in the form of serpents.

Messengers from Moctezuma thrown into irons
Florentine Codex

Many of the post-Conquest accounts which tell of the gifts of Moctezuma to Cortés, describe the mask which belonged with the regalia of the god Quetzalcoatl as being a 'serpent mask'. The description given in Sahagun reads: ' A mask worked in mosaic of turquoise; this mask has a double and twisted snake worked in the same stones whose fold was on the projection of the nose, then the tail was parted from the head and the head with part of the body went above one of the eyes so that it formed an eyebrow, and the tail with a part of the body went over the other eye to form the other eyebrow. This mask was decked with a great and lofty crown, full of rich feathers, very long and beautiful, so that on placing the crown on the head, the mask was placed over the face . . .'

Unfortunately part of this mask is broken away. What remains corresponds closely enough with the description given above, except that both the serpent heads are lost, and it is the two serpent tails which form the eyebrows. However, Sahagun's informants were speaking from memory some years after the Conquest. The plumes of feathers which hang down beside the eye sockets do seem to indicate the 'Feathered Serpent', Quetzalcoatl.

Another god who is sometimes shown with eyes and nose formed from entwined serpents is the rain god Tlaloc, but he would usually, although there are exceptions, have long fang-like teeth; nor would the feathers be consistent with this interpretation. But with the costumes presented to Cortés was one of the god Tlaloc. The two high priests who served the gods Tlaloc and Huitzilopochtli whose shrines were at the top of the Great Temple in Tenochtitlan, were called Quetzalcoatl Totec Tlamacazqui and Quetzalcoatl Tlaloc Tlamacazqui, but we do not know that their regalia in any way symbolized the attributes of the gods whose names they bore.

This mask is reproduced in colour on the front cover

After the entry into Tenochtitlan the Spaniards did of course acquire further treasures, but the greater part of these are said to have been lost on their subsequent flight from the city on *La Noche Triste*, the Night of Sorrows, when the Spaniards threw them into the lake waters to lighten themselves for flight, or carried them with them as they themselves fell into the water dead or dying. Few of them seem ever to have been recovered.

The triumph of the Aztec warriors on that occasion was short-lived. The Spaniards had suffered only a temporary setback. Their vengeance was terrible; the descriptions of the following siege and ultimate surrender of Tenochtitlan make sad reading. An anonymous Aztec poet wrote after the Conquest of the bitter degradations of that time, and ends his poem on a note familiar in Aztec literature, reminding us of the uncertain value of all earthly things:

And all this happened to us.
We saw it,
We marvelled at it.
With this sad and mournful destiny
we saw ourselves afflicted.

The spears lie broken on the streets.
Our hair is torn.
Gone are the roofs of our houses,
their walls red with blood.
Worms crawl across the streets and squares,
brains cling to walls.

Red are the waters,
lurid as tan-bark,
and when we drink
the water tastes of tears.

We beat upon the walls of clay,
our heritage a much rent net.
The shields
could give us no safety.
Roots have we eaten,
chewed water-weed.
With dust and rubble
we stilled our hunger,
with lizards and rats, and worms.
If we saw meat
we ate it almost raw,
seized it impatiently,
swallowed it.

Gold, jade, precious raiment,
quetzal feathers,
everything once of value
has become nothing.

Scene of massacre in the Great Temple at Tenochtitlan during the celebration of the festival of Huitzilopochtli.

After the capture of Tenochtitlan by Cortés and his men, Cortés had to leave the city to deal with the forces sent from Cuba to secure his arrest. During this time he left Pedro de Alvarado as his deputy. The Aztecs were granted permission by the Spaniards to celebrate in the usual way the the festival of their principal god Huitzilopochtli. Alvarado would not allow the imprisoned Moctezuma to attend, perhaps fearing a plot to free him.

The rites began and when the 'dance was loveliest and when song was linked to song' the watching Spaniards rushed forward into the courtyard and slaughtered the celebrants who carried 'nothing in their hands but flowers and feathers'.

Durán, *The History of the Indies of New Spain*, Atlas.

We are told that Moctezuma had made for him images of all animals and birds which he could not have in the menagerie at Tenochtitlan. The few carvings of animals that remain in wood show a very lively style, and carvings of animals are amongst the best of Aztec stone sculpture and lapidary work.

Cortés writes to Charles V in his second letter that Moctezuma kept every kind of bird, all manner of waterfowl and birds of prey and that 'There were certain large rooms in this palace, fitted with great cages, very well constructed, and joined with heavy timbers, in all or most of which were kept lions, tigers, foxes and every kind of cat in considerable numbers. . . . Three hundred other men had charge of these animals and birds.'

Not so impressed was Bernal Díaz who wrote: 'Let me now speak of the infernal noise when the lions and tigers roared and the jackals and the foxes howled and the serpents hissed, it was horrible to listen to and it seemed like a hell.'

The identification of the animals in these descriptions is a little uncertain, but in the eleventh book of Sahagun's 'Florentine Codex', the subject of which is 'Earthly things', there is a long list of the animals and the insects of the kingdom, as well as the plants, which it seems Moctezuma also collected, and the raw materials, the minerals, shells, stones, etc.

. . . the king kept . . . all species and varieties of birds, animals, reptiles and snakes which were brought to him from every province . . . and those which could not be obtained he caused to be depicted in gold and precious stones, likewise sea and fresh-water fish. So no animal of the whole country was wanting here: they were either alive or figured in gold and gems.
Ixtlilxochitl, *Obras Históricas*

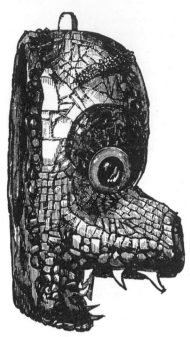

The materials other than turquoise, shell and malachite used in the mosaic work on this small mask have been described as seed pearls, emeralds and garnets. Many such precious and semi-precious stones are listed in the Conquest period inventories, but are rarely found either on specimens in museum collections or in archaeological excavations. It has been questioned that the stones on this piece are of the Aztec period; some of them have certainly been re-set with wax rather than the original gum. Perhaps the analysis of the materials at present in progress will suggest an answer. The animal represented is most frequently described as a monkey, but from some angles strongly suggests a fish head. The teeth are described in old descriptions as 'fish teeth' and 'sharks' teeth'. If the former, then it may be a representation of a particular species. Again it is hoped that current research will solve this query. The shell loop at the top of the mask indicates that it was to be worn as a pendant. There are several descriptions in the inventories of small animal heads with mirrors set into them. A rim of gum

This small figure of a seated jaguar has upon its shoulders a shallow cup-like depression on which there are minute traces of the original gilding. Although badly damaged it is the most animated of the carvings in the collection. It could perhaps have been used as a small offering vessel or a ceremonial mortar; the depression is scarcely deep enough to have been used for a cup.

on the inner side of the head could have held a flat mosaic mirror, and the object would then have been a very pleasing small looking glass to be worn around the neck.

29

Gold jewel with mosaic work centre
Codex Kingsborough

Plan of the Great Temple precinct at
Tenochtitlan: taken from part of the
monumental work of the Franciscan friar
Bernardino de Sahagun (*Codex Matritensis*).
At the centre is the Great Temple itself
with the twin shrines of the gods Tlaloc
and Huitzilopochtli. Moctezuma himself
is said to have been interested in the
religions of other peoples, and the Aztecs
often incorporated the gods of conquered
territories into their existing pantheon.
Sometimes merely by adding the foreign
deity as a new aspect of one of their own
gods; sometimes as new gods in their own
right.

In front of the Great Temple stands the
temple of Quetzalcoatl and *tzompantli* or
'skull rack', where the skulls of sacrificial
victims were skewered onto wooden stakes.
The round stone at the side of the *tzompantli*
was used for a different kind of sacrifice,
wherein a captured warrior was tethered
to the stone and given a wooden sword
edged with tufts of down instead of the
sharp obsidian blades. He had in addition
four sharp stakes which he could hurl at his
adversaries. He fought with a succession
of knights, always including at least two of
each of the great military orders of Eagle
and Jaguar Knights.

At the sides are a prison and the houses
of the priests. Bernal Díaz writes: 'Let us
go on beyond the court to another Cue
(temple) where the great Mexican princes
were buried, where also there were many
idols, and all was full of blood and smoke,
and it had other doorways with hellish
figures, and then near that Cue was
another full of skulls and large bones
arranged in perfect order, which one could
look at but could not count, for there were
too many of them. The skulls were by
themselves and the bones in separate piles.
In that place there were other idols, and in
every Cue house or oratory that I have
mentioned there were priests with long
robes of black cloth. . . . The hair of these
priests was very long and so matted that it
could not be separated or disentangled,
and most of them had their ears scarified,
and their hair was clotted with blood.'

Even jade is shattered,
Even gold is crushed,
Even quetzal plumes are torn . . .
One does not live forever on this earth:
We endure only for an instant!

Song ascribed to king Nezahualcoyotl of Texcoco

30

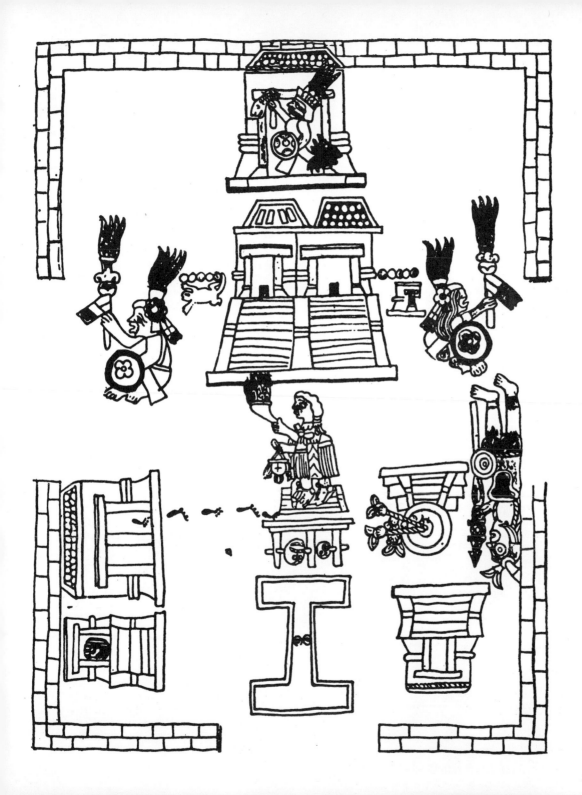

Helmets of wood, some gilded, some decorated with mosaic work appear in the inventories, often described as having crests of plumes, or even complete birds of feather mosaic work to ornament them. It is possibly because it would never have been worn without such adornment that this is not a headdress of a style which can be recognized on sculptures or in the codices. The design in the mosaic work is badly broken away, and sadly there is not, as with some of the other mosaic pieces, such a clear impression of the stones left in the gum, that the original design can quite easily be made out. However, on one side at least it is possible to distinguish two serpents, whose bodies cross at the centre of the helmet. Perhaps they twined round the entire circumference. The inner surface of the helmet is painted green, and there are traces of red pigment on the outer surface.

Item: two coloured pieces of featherwork which are for two pieces of head armour of stone mosaic work, which is mentioned further on . . .

More, another head armour of blue stone mosaic work with twenty gold bells which hang pendent at the border . . .

Item: another head armour of blue stone mosaic work with twenty-five gold bells, and two beads of gold above each bell . . . and a bird of green plumage with the feet, beak and eyes of gold.

Report of the Jewels, Shields, and Clothing sent to the Emperor Charles V from Don Fernando Cortés and the Town Council of Vera Cruz

APPENDIX A

All the examples of turquoise mosaic work now in the British Museum are frequently referred to as belonging to the Christy Collection. As this might lead to confusion in deciding the actual location at any given point in time of the individual pieces, a summary history of the Christy Collection itself might usefully be given.

Henry Christy, born in 1810, died on 4 May, 1865, at La Palisse in France. He had travelled extensively during his lifetime: in northern Europe, America and in the East, and was an inveterate collector. In 1862 he had privately printed a *Catalogue of a collection of ancient and modern stone implements, and of other weapons, tools, and utensils of the aborigines of various countries, in the possession of Henry Christy, F.G.S., F.L.S., &c.* This collection, or such of it as was not in storage, was arranged and catalogued by a friend of Christy's, a Mr Steinhauer of the museum in Copenhagen. The exhibited part was displayed in Christy's rooms at 103 Victoria Street, Westminster. On Christy's death the archaeological and ethnographical collections, along with a sum of money, were bequeathed to four trustees, one of whom was Augustus Wollaston Franks, then Assistant Keeper in the Antiquities Department of the British Museum, who became in the following year Keeper of British and Medieval Antiquities and Ethnography. 'As the best mode of carrying out the intentions of the testator, they decided on offering to the Trustees of the British Museum the collection arranged

by Mr Steinhauer (which was directed not to be dispersed), together with the best selection of objects of a like nature that could be made from the remainder of the collections.' The collection was accepted by the Trustees and temporarily allowed to remain at Victoria Street where six rooms were devoted to display and a catalogue published in 1868.

The money left by Christy was used to purchase additional objects and the collection was also considerably augmented by donations from a great number of sources. Thus, though Christy himself purchased only three examples of Mexican turquoise mosaic (nos. 1–3 in the following list), the 1868 catalogue already includes a fourth (no. 4) which was presented by Mr – later Sir – Augustus Wollaston Franks. The collection was moved to the British Museum in Bloomsbury in 1883.

There follow descriptions of the nine pieces in the order of their acquisition by the British Museum. Included in these descriptions are notes on what little is known of the European history of the objects. This history is at present the subject of research and can be expected to be enlarged upon in the future, although there seems little hope that the histories will ever be completely known.

Attempts are also being made to achieve a much more exact analysis of the materials employed in the manufacture of the mosaics. Moctezuma received turquoise as tribute from various parts of his empire. We know from *Codex Mendoza*, a copy of his tribute list, where turquoise both as a raw material and as mosaic work is illustrated, that from towns in present-day Vera Cruz, he received annually '2 discs of turquoise mosaic'; from towns in modern Guerrero, '1 dish of little turquoise stones'. From a province in Oaxaca came every year '10 middle-sized turquoise masks (mosaic)', made by the skilled Mixtec lapidaries, some of whom may well have lived and traded in Tenochtitlan.

What follows is based upon earlier descriptions and observation and remains necessarily vague in some particulars. The various catalogue numbers which have applied to the pieces are listed at the end of each entry following the number by which the piece is registered in the British Museum.

1 A cedar wood mask, $6\frac{5}{8}$ inches high and $5\frac{7}{8}$ inches wide, the outer surface being completely covered with a mosaic of turquoise. The inner side is thinly coated with red pigment. The eyes and teeth are of white shell. There are pierced squares of shell at each temple.

This mask was bought by Henry Christy at the 1859 sale of the collection of Bram Hertz. It came to the Museum with the Christy Collection in 1865. Hertz's letter to Christy (Appendix B) gives what little is known of its previous history. From this it can be assumed that it was in Italy, probably Florence, until about 1830.

St. 400; C. H. Read, no. 7; Christy catalogue, 1862, I, §i, 80; Hertz sale catalogue, lot 1834

2 A knife, $12\frac{1}{2}$ inches long, with a blade of honey-coloured chalcedony, $2\frac{1}{8}$ inches at its greatest width and $5\frac{5}{8}$ inches in exposed length. The handle is carved in wood and covered with a mosaic of turquoise, malachite, white, pink, purple and orange shell and a few

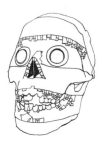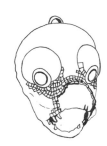

pieces of pearl shell. It represents a crouching figure of a man wearing an eagle headdress the wings of which extend over his shoulders. The blade is held in a socket clutched to the chest of the crouching figure.

This piece too was bought by Christy at the Hertz sale. Its previous history, according to Hertz, is much the same as the mask's (no. 1), and he believed it to have come from the same Florentine collection.

St. 399; Read, no. 2; Christy, I, §i, 79; Hertz, 1835

3 A mask formed of turquoise and lignite mosaic set on a human skull, the back of which has been cut away and the inside covered with soft leather. The skull, according to Read, is of a 30-year-old man. The mosaic forms broad alternating bands of lignite and turquoise and the eyes are of polished convex discs of iron pyrites set in circles of white shell. The nasal opening has been enlarged slightly and inset with slices of pink shell. The width of the mask is $5\frac{3}{4}$ inches; the height, since the jaw is hinged on the leather lining and is movable, is variable but is approximately 8 inches.

This is the third and last example of turquoise mosaic bought by Christy at the Hertz sale. Hertz in his letter mentions that one of the teeth had been stopped, but this tooth is now missing if it ever was really so. The wig Hertz mentions has also disappeared. In the catalogue of the Hertz sale a sentence is inserted following the three lots:

These three objects may be considered unique; there is no record in any catalogue of the great public museums, that such monuments of the ancient Mexican people are in existence.

Hertz's statement that the skull came from a collection in Bruges is interesting. It was taken by Tylor to imply

that it could have been in Belgium continuously from the time of the Conquest until *c.*1845 when Hertz bought it. That Mexican treasure was in that country at a very early date is testified to by Dürer in the passage quoted on p. 8.

St. 401; Read, no. 1; Christy, I, §i, 81; Hertz, 1836

4 A circular piece of wood, $12\frac{1}{4}$ inches in diameter, which is generally taken to be the body of a shield. There is a $\frac{3}{4}$-inch band of bare wood around the edge which contains twenty-four more or less regularly spaced holes presumably, if it is a shield, used for affixing feathers. The central panel of the object has a calendar disc as part of the design. The body of a serpent meanders across the vertical axis, the shape being picked out with simulated beads of gum, some still bearing traces of the gold leaf which once covered them. The head of the serpent is treated in conventional fashion and its tail consists of a turquoise representation of three plumes. Four figures are placed two in the space at each side of the serpent. The vertical axis is marked by a tree, passing behind the serpent and disc, with a lozenge shape at the top enclosing a recumbent figure.

The shield was bought on 26 December 1866 from William Adams, a dealer who said that it had come from Turin.

St. 397a; Read, no. 4

5 An animal head carved in yellowish wood and encrusted with mosaic of turquoise and malachite, with eyes of iron pyrites set in shell. The eyebrows are formed of seed pearls; the inside of the mouth is

covered by a mosaic of garnet sections, and shows some traces of thin gold foil beneath the stones. It is 4 inches high and has a shell loop set in the top. The open mouth contains seven shark or fish teeth.

A. W. Franks presented this piece to the Museum in August 1868 having purchased it from William Adams who said he had got it in North Italy.

St. 400a; Read, no. 6

6 This mask is carved in cedar wood and the face is formed by the intertwining and looping of two serpents. It is just under 7 inches high and the two serpents' bodies are in different shades of turquoise. The teeth are of shell and the rattles of the serpents seem to have been gilded.

The mask was bought from the Demidoff sale in Paris in 1870 and its immediately prior history is unknown. Lehmann, however, ventures the assumption that it is the otherwise missing mask referred to in the 1640–5 Medici inventory as '*Una maschera di legno Indiana, commessa di turchine laguale notasi che nel di 31 Agosto 1656 venne data ad Anton Francesco Tofani, custode dell' armaria*'.

N.N.; Read, no. 3; Demidoff sale catalogue, lot 475

7 A seated figure of a jaguar with a cup-like receptacle on its back. It is just under 7 inches high and the mosaic covering is mostly turquoise with some pink shell, malachite and iron pyrites. The cup shows some traces of gilt. The figure itself is carved from pale brown wood.

A. W. Franks bought it from Joseph Mayer, the famous Liverpool collector, and presented it to the Museum on 19 March 1877. Mr Mayer gave no previous history for it.

+165; Read, no. 8

8 A wooden helmet, 8 inches across, with two beak-like projections once covered, except for the outer faces and the lower inside parts (which show traces of red colour), with a mosaic of turquoise, malachite, pearl shell and pink shell. A good many of the stones are missing but those that remain clearly define on one side the intertwining bodies of two serpents. The inside is painted green.

The helmet was presented to the Museum on 15 December 1893 by A. W. Franks who had bought it at the Bateman sale. It was bought by one W. Chaffers in Paris in 1854 and was in Bateman's hands at least by 1885.

+6382; Read, no number, first section of text

9 A pendant ornament in the form of a double-headed serpent, $17\frac{1}{8}$ inches long. It is carved out of wood which is hollowed out at the back along the coils of the body so that it is U-shaped in section. The outer surface of the body is covered with a mosaic of turquoise, slightly larger and more irregular pieces forming a line along the centre. The heads are entirely covered with mosaic, mostly of turquoise but with some features – the gums, nostrils and a band across the nose – picked out in red shell. The teeth are of white shell. There are holes at the tops of the two loops for suspension.

This piece was purchased from the Duchessa Massimo through Lord Walsingham with money from the Christy Fund in September 1894.

1894–634; Read, no. 6

APPENDIX B

There follows a transcription of a letter to Henry Christy from Bram Hertz at whose sale Christy bought the three pieces of mosaic now in the British Museum which he himself acquired (nos. 1–3). Hertz's collection, then in the hands of Joseph Mayer of Liverpool, was sold at Sotheby and Wilkinsons in 1859. The catalogue of the sale was entitled: *Catalogue of the celebrated and well-known collection of Assyrian, Babylonian, Egyptian, Greek, Etruscan, Roman, Indian, Peruvian, Mexican & Chinese antiquities formed by B. Hertz, corresponding member of the Archaeological Institute at Rome, now the property of Joseph Mayer, Esq. of Liverpool which will be sold by auction by Messrs. S. Leigh Sotheby & John Wilkinson on 7 February 1859 and 15 days following.* The letter thus predates the sale and is presumably in response to general enquiries made by Christy before he himself possessed any articles of turquoise mosaic.

> 40, Neue Maynzer Strasse
> Frankfort a/m
> 5th Febr 1858

My Dear Sir,

I came this morning in possession of your favour of the 2nd inst and will not lose a moment to give you the desired explanation.

The Mexican Turquoise mask nor the other articles were sold at Christie & Manson's;

The mask and the sacrificial knife belonged to a celebrated collection at Florence of which however I have forgotten the name.–The sale of the said collection took place some twenty odd years ago, and the mask was acquired by a certain Descriever who at the time was travelling as courier with an English familly [*sic*]

and settled afterwards as a curiosity dealer in London. When he brought the said mask over he asked the large sum of £300 for it, however I got it from him in exchange and it stood me about £80.

Some time after I found the sacrificial knife at Mr Pratts in New Bond Street who brought this also from Venice; it was very singular and fortunate that these two articles having belonged to the same collection, should be united again through two different channels.

I found in the case containing the mask a memorandum which stated that it belonged to a convent of nuns at Mozza and that it was of Egyptian origin, this latter assertion I doubted very much, and declared it to be Mexican in which opinion I was confirmed by the acquisition of the knife, as the handle of this is of undoubted Mexican design.

I was requested by some gentleman to exhibit the aforesaid two articles at the Royal Asiatic Society, which I did; Professor Wilson was in the chair, who doubted them to be of Mexican origin, as he argued that no Turquoise were found in Mexico, I replied that I was aware of that, but that Mexicans had communications with other countries, who might have supplied the material for these articles.

Some time after my opinion was confirmed by a member of the Society, who discovered in a book that in the service of the Mexican God Tlaloc such masks and sacrificial knives were used in human sacrifices.–This gentleman whose name I have forgotten, held afterwards at public institutions lectures on ancient Mexico and I lent him the mask and knife as an illustration to his lectures.

The skull was in a Collection at Bruges which was sold about 12 years ago, as also a wig which was described as a scalp. On the scull [*sic*] there is a material which is called obsidian, and which is found in great abundance in Mexico. I showed this scull to a french dentist who found that one of the teeth is stopped, which is very remarkable.

The nrs 128, 129, 130 were in the Poniatowsky's Collection and were sold about twenty years ago at Christies & Manson. I recollect I gave £10 for the no 128.

Believe me my dear Sir
Ever your's
B Hertz

H. Christy Esqre London

BIBLIOGRAPHY

Aldrovanus, Ulysses, *Musaeum metallicum*, Bologna, 1648

Alva Ixtlilxochitl, Fernando de, *Obras Históricas*, Mexico, 1829

Anglerius, Peter Martyr, *De Orbe Novo*, trans. F. A. MacNutt, 2 vols., New York, 1912

Barlow, R. H., *The extent of the empire of the Culhua Mexica*, Ibero-Americana: 28, Berkeley and Los Angeles, 1949

Bernal, Ignacio, *Mexico before Cortez*, trans. W. Barnstone, New York, 1963

Bray, Warwick, *Everyday life of the Aztecs*, London, 1968

British Museum, *Guide to the Christy Collection . . . temporarily placed at 103 Victoria Street, Westminster*, London, 1868

Caso, Alfonso, *The Aztecs: People of the Sun*, Norman, 1958

Coe, Michael D., *Mexico*, London, no date

Cooper Clark, James, *Codex Mendoza*, London, 1938

Cortés, Hernando, *Letters of Cortes*, trans. F. A. MacNutt, 2 vols., New York, 1908

Díaz, Bernal del Castillo, *The True History of the Conquest of New Spain*, trans. A. P. Maudslay, London, 1908–16

Gómara, Francisco, López de, *Cortés, the life of the Conqueror, by his secretary*, trans. L. B. Simpson, Berkeley and Los Angeles, 1964

Hertz, Bram, *Catalogue of a collection . . .*, London, 1851

Joyce, T. A., *A short guide to the American antiquities in the British Museum*, London, 1912

Joyce, T. A., *Mexican archaeology*, London, 1914

Lehmann, Walter, 'Altmexikanische Mosaiken und die Geschenke König Motecuzomas und Cortes', in *Globus*, Bd. XC, no. 20, 1906

Lehmann, Walter, 'Die altmexikanischen Mosaiken der ethnographischen Museums in Kopenhagen', in *Globus*, Bd. XCI, no. 21, 1907

León-Portilla, Miguel, ed., *The broken spears, the Aztec account of the Conquest of Mexico*, trans. L. Kemp, London, 1962

León-Portilla, Miguel, *Aztec thought and culture*, trans. J. E. Davis, Norman, 1963

León-Portilla, Miguel, *Pre-Columbian literatures of Mexico*, trans. G. Lobanov and author, Norman, 1969

Peterson, Frederick, *Ancient Mexico*, London, 1959

Pigorini, L., 'Gli antichi ogetti messicani incrostati di mosaico esistanti nel Museo preistorico ed etnografico di Roma' in *Atti della R, Acc. dei Lincei*, third series, vol. 12, Rome, 1885

Prescott, William, *The Conquest of Mexico* (illustrations by K. Henderson), London, 1922

Read, Charles Hercules, *On an ancient Mexican head-piece coated with mosaic*, London, 1895

Sahagun, Fray Bernardino de, *General History of the Things of New Spain*, trans. A. J. O. Anderson and C. E. Dibble, 9 vols., Santa Fe, 1950–

Sahagun, Fray Bernardino de, *Historia General de las Cosas de Nueva Espana*, ed. A. M. Garibay K, 4 vols., Mexico, 1969

Saville, Marshall H., *The earliest notices concerning the Conquest of Mexico by Cortés in 1519*, New York, 1920

Saville, Marshall H., *Turquoise Mosaic Art in Ancient Mexico*, New York, 1922

Seler, Eduard, 'Über szenische Darstellungen auf altmexikanischen Mosaiken', in *Gesammelte Abhandlungen zur Amerikanischen Sprach- und Altertumskunde*, Bd. 4, Berlin, 1923

Soustelle, Jacques, *The daily life of the Aztecs*, London, 1961

Steinhauer, M., *Catalogue of a collection of ancient and modern stone implements . . . in the possession of Henry Christy*, London, 1862

Stevens, Edward T., *Flint Chips*, London, 1870

Tylor, Edward B., *Anahuac*, London, 1861

NOTES

[1] From the codices of both pre- and post-Conquest periods an impression can be gained of the textiles, costumes and jewellery, etc. *Codex Magliabecchiano* has some excellent illustrations of robes worn for various festivals; *Codex Mendoza* illustrates particularly well the costumes and shields of warriors; *Codex Kingsborough* has paintings of jewellery.

[2] This suggestion is taken from the work of one of the best-known authorities on Aztec culture, Jacques Soustelle. In his book *Arts of Ancient Mexico*, London, 1966, he writes: 'It is said that Benvenuto Cellini, seeing the magnificent fish with gold and silver scales which Charles V had received from Mexico and then given as a present to the Pope, cried out in admiration that he could not understand how the Mexican goldsmiths had been able to attain such a standard of perfection.'

[3] Two interesting articles which illustrate Mexican stone carvings placed in elaborate European settings are worth mentioning. Both the pieces concerned are small stone masks which could not be broken down like composite jewellery. The contrast in styles is bizarre.

a) Callegari, G. V., 'Suppellettile precolombiana del Museo Nazionale d'Antropologia ed Etnologia di Firenze', in *Le Vie d'Italia e dell' America Latina*, Fascicolo VI, Giugno 1932–X.

b) Heikamp, D. and F. Anders, 'Mexikanische Altertümer aus süddeutschen Kunstkammern', in *Pantheon*, III, xxviii, May/June 1970.

Alfred Percival Maudslay, in the description of the turquoise mosaics in the British Museum appended to the first volume of his translation of Bernal Díaz del Castillo's 'The true History of the Conquest of New Spain' (published by the Hakluyt Society, 1908–1916), has the following note written in connection with the collection of mosaics brought together in the Ethnographical Museum in Rome by Professor L. Pigorini: 'However, the greater number of them up to the years 1819–21 were registered in the Florentine Museum and with the title *Maschere e strumenti de popoli barbari*, and were partly sent thence to the *Officina delle pietre dure* in that city to be broken up and used for mosaic work, being *Maschere di cattivi turchesi!*' Cf. also M. Coe, *Mexico*, no date, – 'The stupendous collection of mosaic pieces once in the hands of Charles V and now in the British Museum and in Florence bear eloquent testimony to late Mexican workmanship in this medium, although most examples were consumed in the *pietre dure* "laboratories" in the early nineteenth century.'

[4] Fray Bernardino de Sahagun, *General History of the Things of New Spain*.

[5] Peter Martyr, *De Orbe Novo*.

[6] Bernal Díaz del Castillo, *The True History of the Conquest of New Spain*.

[7] Francisco López de Gómara, *Istoria de la Conquista de Mexico*.

[8] Hernan Cortés, *Second letter to the Emperor Charles V*.

[9] William Prescott, *The Conquest of Mexico*.

[10] An anonymous Aztec poet.

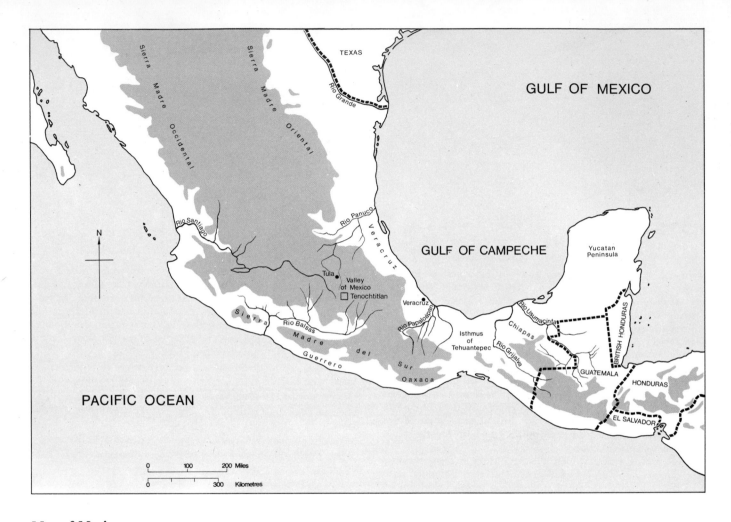

Map of Mexico